RENELE AWONO

The Process of Purpose

AN IN DEPTH BIBLE STUDY OF GOD USING ORDINARY PEOPLE TO WALK IN EXTRAORDINARY PURPOSE

© 2021 by Renele Awono
The Process of Purpose

All rights reserved. No portion of this book may be reproduced, stored in a retrieval system, or transmitted in any form or by means-electronic, mechanical, photocopy, recording, scanning, or other-except for brief quotations in critical reviews or articles, without prior permission of the publisher.

Unless otherwise noted, Scriptures used in this volume are taken from the Holy Bible, the New King James Version®. Copyright © 1982 by Thomas Nelson. Used by permission. All rights reserved.

Scripture quotations designated ESV are from The Holy Bible, English Standard Version ®, copyright © 2001 by Crossway Bibles, a publishing ministry of Good News Publishers. Used by permission. All rights reserved.

Scriptures noted (NIV) are taken from the Holy Bible, New International Version®, NIV® Copyright ©1973, 1978, 1984, 2011 by Biblica, Inc.® Used by permission. All rights reserved worldwide.

Scripture taken from the New King James Version®. Copyright © 1982 by Thomas Nelson, Inc. Used by permission. All rights reserved.

Scriptures noted (MSG) are taken from the Holy Bible, The Message, Copyright © 1993, 1994, 1995, 1996, 2000, 2001, 2002 by Eugene H. Peterson.

Scriptures noted (AMP) are taken from the Holy Bible, Amplified Bible, Copyright © 2015 by The Lockman Foundation, La Habra, CA 90631. All rights reserved.

Scriptures noted (NLT) are taken from the Holy Bible, New Living Translation, copyright © 1996, 2004, 2015 by Tyndale House Foundation. Used by permission of Tyndale House Publishers Inc., Carol Stream, Illinois 60188. All rights reserved.

Paperback:
ISBN-13: 978-1-7353526-2-6
Library of Congress Control Number:

copyright notice

All rights reserved.
No part of this publication may be reproduced, distributed, or transmitted in any form or by any means, including photocopying, recording, or other electronic or mechanical methods, without the prior written permission of the publisher, except in the case of brief quotations embodied in critical reviews and certain other noncommercial uses permitted by copyright law.

Copyright © 2021 by Renele Awono

Hi, I'm Renele!

Since the very beginning of time God has been moving you into purpose. I am beyond excited at what He is doing in your life in Jesus name.

I am an author, coach/consultant, wife & mother of 3 and counting! I am walking in the destiny that God declared for me and I'm loving it! I get to see lives changed, families delivered, communities and nations transformed as a result of who God created me to be! It's your time to shine, by moving into what God called you to do! So, tag your it!

It is no accident that you found this bible study, my prayer is that you receive everything God intended for you to receive as you read!

INSTAGRAM | FACEBOOK

Welcome!

My name is Renele Awono, author of "Fearfully & Wonderfully Created" & "The Process of Purpose", an In Depth Bible Study that inspires a deeper understanding of walking in purpose. The Bible Study was inspired by the Holy Spirit and is an extension of my book, Fearfully and Wonderfully Created. "The Process of Purpose" is a deep dive into Gods invitation for us to step into the divine plan that He designed for us. As you walk through this journey you will learn more about the **Preparation** necessary for the fulfillment of destiny, the **Positioning** that God is setting you up for, His **Purpose** & why you have to say yes, finally, we will explore the One who **Perfectly** implemented His purpose.

I want to congratulate you in making the decision to dig deeper on your journey to BE all and DO all that God created you for. God has always had an amazing plan for your life and He is so excited that you have accepted His invitation to seek out that which He designed for you from the very beginning of time.

It has been a long time theme in my life to know and fully understand what I am here on earth for. I've always wanted to know why I was born. My mom had miscarriages before & after me, why was I the one that survived? As I began to intentionally seek God, He began to reveal pieces of the puzzle to me so that I would have a clearer picture as to what my purpose was here on earth. My focus then shifted to having a deep desire to BE all and DO all He created me for.

It is amazing when God reveals His intentions for your life. Finally, He shifted me again from not only wanting to do what I was purposed for, but helping others fulfill their purpose.

Fearfully & Wonderfully Created, was born out of the frustration of life experiences that seemed to always detour me away from doing what I was created for. God pressed upon my heart that this was not only my story, but the story of many others. There are countless others that have understood the promises of God and yet they have not experienced them in their lives. Fearfully & Wonderfully Created is a transparent look at our identity in Christ, God's intention for us, how to overcome obstacles we often face & ways we can identify and walk out our purpose. In Christ we overcome, the Bible says that we are more than conquers in (Romans 8:37). Each of us have unique lived experiences that God can turn around and use for our good. We have a wonderful opportunity to partner with Christ allowing Him to use what we have been through and make it into something beautiful.

It is my desire that as you go through this study that God will begin to give you His perspective on walking in your purpose. My prayer is that divine acceleration, wisdom and transformation for your destiny begins to flood your life. There are no coincidences in God, you are at the right moment in destiny to begin your journey with the King which will change your life forever, if you allow it.

How to use this Study

This study was designed for you to capture what the Lord is speaking to you about your destiny! Many of the bible verses addressed are directly within the text for ease of study. This study is full of opportunities to assist you in moving toward your purpose. Take a moment to get familiar with the sections in this in depth study.

PURPOSE OF THIS MODULE — Quick references points to help you understand what you will be learning about in each module.

HOLY SPIRIT WHISPERS — As you hear from the Lord, you will be able to write those precious words down in the space provided.

NOTES — A convenient space to jot down points that you would like to ponder upon at a later time.

Reflection Questions — After each module you will find reflection questions to assist in processing the information within the module as it pertains to your purpose.

It's time to MOVE forward! — Move Forward, is a call to action at the end of each module. These sections are designed to help you to begin to activate your move into destiny.

The Purpose Challenge was created to lead you into targeted times of prayer and action to help catapult you into what God created you to do.

This Prayer Treasury are short prayer prompts were designed to lead you into deeper times of intimacy with God.

the foundation

From the beginning God has set His intentions on us for good, in fact, it was His good pleasure to give us His kingdom. He specifically created us for the purpose of partnering with Him in fulfilling His plan in the earth. It's important that we have an understanding of this so that we can move forward, partnering with Him in wisdom and truth.

Jeremiah, the prophet explained this in great detail. He states that, "Before I formed thee in the belly I knew thee; and before thou camest forth out of the womb I sanctified thee, and I ordained thee a prophet unto the nations." (Jeremiah 1:5) This gives an understanding that we were predestined, cleansed from every sin we would ever commit, and set apart by God for His specific purposes. 2 Peter 1:3 further explains, for His divine power has granted to us everything pertaining to life and godliness, through the true knowledge of Him who called us by His own glory and excellence. Our destiny was put in place and everything that we would need to fulfill it had already been given to us.

Walking out these foundational truths require us to CHOOSE Christ. We must choose to accept Christ as our Savior to receive the benefits, purposes & plans that God preordained for us. Once we accept Christ we can then make daily choices to partner with God to be what He created us to be. These choices will require us to make sacrifices and walk in the Spirit of God to fulfill ALL He created us to be. We must remember that our Creator knows best...after all He created us.

The Process of Purpose

QUICK OVERVIEW

Stepping into your destiny is no small task, below you will find a brief overview to reference as you are on your journey to purpose.

The Invitation

God gives us an invitation to partner with the plans that He created for us from the beginning of time.

The Preparation

All throughout your life God has been preparing you for something great, whether you know it or not.

The Purpose

As you walk out destiny you are accomplishing far more than you know. There are eternal purposes being accomplished as well.

The Positioning

God has a way of leading us into our destiny, through various means. Pay attention, you have been placed for such a time as this!

The Perfection

We are not without help when it comes to walking out or destiny. God sent us the perfect example, Jesus!

The Response

You have the invitation to co-partner with God in this earth...how will you respond?

Module Outline

01 The Invitation

02 The Preparation

03 The Positioning

04 The Positioning Pt. 2

04 The Purpose

05 The Perfection

06 The Response

01

The Invitation

YOU HAVE BEEN INVITED SINCE THE BEGINNING OF TIME, HOW WILL YOU RESPOND?

The Invitation

There is an invitation given to us by God to step into the plans He has for us. Often times, we don't know what those plans are or even where to start. It starts with His invitation. As discussed in Fearfully & Wonderfully Created, before time began He designed you with a purpose on purpose! Ephesians 2:10 explains this so well,

10 *For we are His workmanship, created in Christ Jesus for good works, which God prepared beforehand that we should walk in them!*

The blueprint for what He desires has been drawn up, but of course, it's up to us to choose His plans. Prayerfully after you complete this bible study you will have a greater courage to take a leap of faith into the purpose you were created for.

PURPOSE OF THIS MODULE
• To understand God's invitation into destiny
• To understand how He will give you wisdom for the journey
• The get an understanding of what "Purpose" is

So you may be wondering what exactly is the "Invitation"? The "Invitation" is the calling or purpose that God has created you for, it's is the sole reason for which you exist. *Purpose* is defined as the reason for which something is done or created or for which something exists. [1] Similarly, a *calling* is a strong urge toward a particular way of life or career; a vocation. [2]

God intentionally, with great love and care, formed you in your mothers womb and even at that time, purpose was taking shape. King David explains it like this in Psalms 139:13-16,

13 For You formed my inward parts; You covered me in my mother's womb. *14 I will praise You, for I am fearfully and wonderfully made; Marvelous are Your works, And that my soul knows very well.* *15 My frame was not hidden from You, when I was made in secret, and skillfully wrought in the lowest parts of the earth. 16 Your eyes saw my substance, being yet unformed. And in Your book they all were written, the days fashioned for me, when as yet there were none of them.*

Verse *16* *explains that the days of your life were already written in your book, even though they had not yet come to past.*

You see, there was an intricate blueprint already created for your life, however you have a choice to accept or decline the plans God has for you. Yes, you have a choice!

I'm not sure about you but I want to do all and be all that I was created for! So why did He do that, why did He design us with a plan already in mind? Genesis 1:26 explains,

26 Then God said, " Let us make man in Our image, according to Our likeness; let them have dominion over the fish of the sea, over the birds of the air, and over the cattle, over all the earth and over every creeping thing that creeps on the earth.

We have a purpose which is clearly defined here on a larger scale. God's plan was to give us to RULE in the earth. We have dominion on earth because of Jesus to do and be all that He created us to be and show forth the will of God in the earth.

With this delegated authority, we have been "Invited" to a higher calling. The invitation is to develop a deeper relationship with God, walk out His purposes in your life and in the lives of others and to bring the manifestation of the Kingdom of God in the earth.

Let's explore what happens when ordinary people like you and I say, "Yes," in response to God's invitation.

The Revelator

John the Revelator comes to mind. John, often called the "Beloved" of Christ, was the writer of the Gospel of John, 1st, 2nd, 3rd John & the book of Revelation. Throughout John's life he received several invitations from God.

He was invited to become an apostle of Jesus Christ and he was the only one that stayed close to Jesus at the Cross. Much of what John wrote was what he saw and experienced while with Jesus and through the revelation the Holy Spirit on the isle of Patmos.

However, when we get to Revelation chapter 4 we see a distinct invitation, while yet another dimension of revelation is stirring. John recalls a vision that the Lord showed him,

1 After this I looked and saw a door standing open in heaven. And the voice I had previously heard speak to me like a trumpet was saying, "Come up here, and I will show you what must happen after these things." (Revelation 4:1)

HOLY SPIRIT WHISPERS

Up until this point God spoke to John about things that were happening presently. This was invitation to a deeper layer of revelation. In the next phase of this invitation, He desired to elevate John from just knowing what was presently happening to having knowledge of things to come.

This bible study is an invitation from the Lord for you to come up higher & join Him at the banquet to eat from His table. It's an invitation to let Him download supernatural secrets to you, the mysteries from the Kingdom. Yes, there are secrets that He wants to reveal to you! Each time John accepted the invitation the Holy Spirit would give more opportunities for deeper revelation.

2 *It is the glory of God to conceal things, but the glory of kings is to search things out. (Prov. 25:2.)*

This scripture explains the mystery of how the Kingdom operates, God intentionally conceals His secrets for us to dig deep and search them out, it's His way of developing a relationship with us. As we seek and search we draw nearer and become closer to Him. He promises that He will give us hidden treasures, riches stored in secret places, so that we may know that He is the LORD, the God of Israel, who summons us by name. (*Isaiah 45:3*)

HOLY SPIRIT WHISPERS

The Prophet

NOTES

Elijah, the prophet, was also one who sought God. He was one stood in the presence of the Lord and received great revelation. He gave Elijah step by step instructions and detailed plans to follow. Elijah is known for :

- His powerful witness
- Miracles performed
- Relentless devotion God

Elijah's purpose was to silence false prophets, evil kings and tear down false gods that were set up to lead Israel astray. Now, that was a difficult purpose! Elijah was created & specifically designed for his assignment. He intentionally drew close to God, so close that he stood in His presence.

1** Now Elijah the Tishbite, who was of the settlers of Gilead, said to Ahab, "As the LORD, the God of Israel lives,* ***before whom I stand*, surely there shall be neither dew nor rain these years, except by my word. (1 Kings 17:1)*

So what does it exactly mean to stand before the Lord? Lee Ann Rubsam in her article, The Lord God …Before Whom I Stand (Part 2), explains it like this:

"It is standing at attention before Him in His throne room as His servant, watching for the least gesture of His hand or the least eye contact, knowing what He wants and moving to do it. She further explains, that this requires an acute sensitivity to Him.

2 Behold, as the eyes of servants look unto the hand of their masters, and as the eyes of a maiden unto the hand of her mistress; so our eyes wait upon the LORD our God
(Psalms 123:2)

It means having face-to-face relationship with God (intimacy). It means to be one who is invited into His war council room, to take counsel with Him for His strategies. It is a place of honor, and is not to be taken casually.

Although it is every believer's potential privilege, not everyone achieves this kind of intimacy with the Lord. It is not an easy place to come into. It requires a total abandon of all self into the Lords hands.

It involves the painful refining at His hand.[3]

When Elijah stood in the presence of the Lord he received specific instructions about how to be victorious in the midst of the enemies of God. The enemies against Elijah and God were powerful people the could have done great harm and even killed him but God protected and sustained him. Take some time to read the story of Elijah, he was victorious even when he felt as if was alone. In I Kings chapters 17-18, it is clear that God was with Elijah, He gives him instructions on where to travel, He makes provision for him. We see God's provision as Elijah's thirst was quenched by the brook and as he was fed by a raven and a widow.

We also see God's backing in other instances such as when he obeyed God's instructions to pronounce the judgment of no rain, when he stood against 450 false prophets of Baal & King Ahab and when he promised the widow that her flour and oil would not run dry until the famine ceased. All of these events were miraculous and displayed the power of God working in the life of Elijah.

God was also with Elijah when the widows son was sick & died. Gods power was also at work when Elijah told Ahab to prepare his chariot and ride before the rain prevented him, this happened after there had be no rain for 3 years and was all part of the purpose that Elijah was created for. Keep in mind that Elijah had the free will to refuse the invitation of the Lord, thank God that he did not. God will back you up as you move into the purpose that has designed for you.

The Prophet

Isaiah was another prophet that stood in the council of God and received wisdom. Isaiah's role was to predict the coming of the Messiah as the Ultimate Leader. God spoke to Isaiah through visions about the future and gave him warnings of impeding judgment for nations.

The powerful revelations that Isaiah received included the depth of understanding about the reign of the Messiah, His suffering and His Kingdom, noted in Isaiah 53; how the Holy Spirit would empower the Messiah, in Isaiah 11:2-5; and the character of the Messiah explained in Isaiah 42:1-4.

THE MESSIAH'S REIGN, SUFFERING & KINGDOM

1 Who has believed our message and to whom has the arm of the Lord been revealed? 2 He grew up before him like a tender shoot, and like a root out of dry ground. He had no beauty or majesty to attract us to him, nothing in his appearance that we should desire him. 3 He was despised and rejected by mankind, a man of suffering, and familiar with pain. Like one from whom people hide their faces he was despised, and we held him in low esteem. 4 Surely he took up our pain and bore our suffering, yet we considered him punished by God, stricken by him, and afflicted.5 But he was pierced for our transgressions, he was crushed for our iniquities; the punishment that brought us peace was on him, and by his wounds we are healed. 6 We all, like sheep, have gone astray, each of us has turned to our own way;

and the Lord has laid on him the iniquity of us all. **7** *He was oppressed and afflicted, yet he did not open his mouth; he was led like a lamb to the slaughter, and as a sheep before its shearers is silent, so he did not open his mouth.* **8** *By oppression and judgment he was taken away. Yet who of his generation protested? For he was cut off from the land of the living; for the transgression of my people he was punished.* **9** *He was assigned a grave with the wicked, and with the rich in his death, though he had done no violence, nor was any deceit in his mouth.* **10** *Yet it was the Lord's will to crush him and cause him to suffer, and though the Lord makes his life an offering for sin, he will see his offspring and prolong his days, and the will of the Lord.* **11** *After he has suffered, he will see the light of life and be satisfied; by his knowledge my righteous servant will justify many, and he will bear their iniquities.* **12** *Therefore I will give him a portion among the great, and he will divide the spoils with the strong, because he poured out his life unto death, and was numbered with the transgressors. For he bore the sin of many, and made intercession for the transgressors.*
 (Isaiah 53)

NOTES

THE EMPOWERMENT OF THE MESSIAH BY THE HOLY SPIRIT

1 The Spirit of the Lord will rest on him the Spirit of wisdom and of understanding, the Spirit of counsel and of might, the Spirit of the knowledge and fear of the Lord. 3 and he will delight in the fear of the Lord. He will not judge by what he sees with his eyes, or decide by what he hears with his ears; 4 but with righteousness he will judge the needy,
with justice he will give decisions for the poor of the earth. He will strike the earth with the rod of his mouth; with the breath of his lips he will slay the wicked. 5 Righteousness will be his belt and faithfulness the sash around his waist. (Isaiah 11:2-5)

THE CHARACTER OF THE MESSIAH

1 Here is my servant, whom I uphold, my chosen one in whom I delight; I will put my Spirit on him, and he will bring justice to the nations. 2 He will not shout or cry out, or raise his voice in the streets. 3 A bruised reed he will not break, and a smoldering wick he will not snuff out. In faithfulness he will bring forth justice; 4 he will not falter or be discouraged till he establishes justice on earth. In his teaching the islands will put their hope. (Isaiah 42:1-4)

Take a few moments to read those passages to get a feel for the depth of revelation that was given to a mere man, a human who was frail and weak in comparison to God, just like you and I. I believe if we had the opportunity to ask Isaiah what the cost of his acceptance to the invitation was, he would say that it cost him everything. I also believe that in the same breath he would said he would do it all over again because it was worth it.

Wisdom

Wisdom is priceless, the revelation from the only true God cannot be compared to anything that we possess here on earth. As we respond with our "YES" to His invitation, there are endless resources available to us for walking out our God ordained purpose. As we develop true intimacy with God we receive more than we could ever imagine, we receive His wisdom as the prudent & all knowing God, His instructions, strategy, encouragement, resources and so much more. A friend shared this passage of scripture with me and it was so powerful, I felt led to share it with you to the demonstrate the infinite wisdom of God.

As you read beyond the surface parable, look deep into the details of His instructions.

23 Hear my voice, listen to my words, and pay close attention to my parable. 24 Does a farmer plow continually at planting time and never plant a crop? Does he continually break open the clods of the ground and never sow his seed? 25 Once he has leveled its surface, does he not sow dill and cumin, planting his wheat in rows, his barley in its proper place, and his rye in a patch. 26 Yes, his God has instructed him and taught him the right way of farming the land. 27 Dill, a small seed, is not threshed with a threshing sledge, nor is a wagon wheel rolled over cumin. Dill is beaten with a rod and cumin with a stick. 28 Grain is crushed and milled for bread, but it is not threshed endlessly. One drives the wagon's wheels over it, but his horses' hooves do not pulverize it.

Using the metaphor of a farmer, Jesus tells His disciples to pay close attention to what He is getting ready to share with them. He lets them know that if they want results they cannot continually do the same thing... repeated efforts will not bring the results you desire. You must take action, not aimlessly, but God inspired actions that will yield results. He explains that there is a process, a pattern that must be followed in order reach the desired outcome of reaping a harvest. Jesus goes on to explain that God is the one that gives the explicit instruction on how to go about the tasks correctly.

HOLY SPIRIT WHISPERS

Then Jesus begins to display His wise counsel, letting the disciples know that each situation, project, assignment may not be handled the same way every time. It takes the unfathomable wisdom of God to lead us into purpose, into what He created us for from the beginning of time. He designed every nuance of your purpose, accept the invitation and let Him lead you into the fulfillment of your destiny.

NOTES

Reflection Questions

In a quiet place reflect on what you are feeling, what stood out to you in this module and what the Lord spoke to you. Take some time to answer the questions below.

HAVE YOU EVER THOUGHT ABOUT FULFILLING YOUR DESTINY? WHY OR WHY NOT?

HAVE YOU ACCEPTED HIS INVITATION TO WALK IN YOUR PURPOSE? WHY OR WHY NOT?

DO YOU CURRENTLY HAVE A RELATIONSHIP WITH JESUS CHRIST? EXPLAIN

Reflection Questions
CONTINUED

WHAT IS YOUR PURPOSE?

WAS THE PREVIOUS QUESTION ABOUT PURPOSE DIFFICULT FOR YOU TO ANSWER? WHY OR WHY NOT?

IN WHAT WAYS ARE YOU CURRENTLY FULFILLING THE CALL ON YOUR LIFE? ARE YOU GROWING IN YOUR CALLING OR FEELING STAGNANT?

It's time to MOVE forward!

The first step in moving forward is to make sure that you are in alignment with God. This is done initially by making sure you have a relationship with Christ. If you have never made a commitment to Jesus Christ or if you have asked Him into your life but have not been living according to His will it is important that you start there. Secondly, often times there are mindsets that we have that are not consistent with God's truth. For example, you may have been told all of your life that you were "stupid". God says that you are Fearfully & Wonderfully made, magnificently designed. You will need to examine your life and get rid of those mindsets. Finally, begin to learn, understand & apply God's truth to your life.

Commit /Re-Commit

If you have not asked Christ into your heart or if you have not acknowledged the God as Lord over you life take a moment to pray the prayer of salvation. This will allow God to realign you will His original purpose for your life.

Undo Faulty Foundations

According to what you just learned, begin to pray that any lies you have believed about God, your destiny & yourself be destroyed. Let Gods truth in those areas begin to work in your life.

Agree with His Truth

Begin to re-read the scriptures in this Module & seek out other scriptures that explain God's will for your life. As you agree with the Word of God His truth in your life will be established.

**ACCEPT HIS INVITATION &
CO-CREATE WITH GOD**

...Come up here and I will show you what must happen after these things

REVELATION 4:1

THE PROCESS OF PURPOSE

The Preparation

DID YOU KNOW THAT YOU ARE BEING PREPARED FOR DESTINY EVEN IF YOU DON'T KNOW WHAT THAT DESTINY IS?

02

The Preparation

Generally when planning a wedding the couple will send out a "Save the Date" to let loved ones know of the upcoming celebration so that they will calendar the event. Once the official invitation arrives it requires a response from you, an "RSVP". When you submit your response, you then prepare for the upcoming celebration. There are also stages that we must go through when we give our "Yes" to the Lord.

PURPOSE OF THIS MODULE

- To understand the importance of being prepared

- To learn why God takes us through preparation

- To study the lives of others that God has taken through the process of preparation

- To learn how God uses our life experiences to prepare us

Esther
Saves a Nation

While composing this Bible study, the Lord placed on my heart to delve into the story of Esther. Preparation is key, Esther, a young virgin girl, will give us more insight into the importance of preparation. She was an orphan who was in the care of her uncle Mordecai, due to the passing away of her parents. A decree went out from the King that he desired young beautiful virgins, one of which would replace the dethroned queen, Vashti. Caught up in the search for virgins for the King, Esther was taken. However, unbeknownst to Esther preparations had already begun to fulfill her destiny. In the process she was removed from that which was familiar, into a foreign environment and away from her relatives. Little did she know, that her destiny was to prevent the genocide of her people, the Jews. Many times we go throughout life having bits and pieces of the plan of God for our lives, yet all the while we are being prepared for something greater.

Esther was very humble and listened intently to her uncles instructions not to tell anyone what her race was. As she was in the process to go before the King, she was being cleansed for 1 year and six months with the oil of myrrh & six months with perfumes and beauty treatments, under the custody of Hegai. Hegai was the King's eunuch and overseer of the women's house. The scriptures tell us that Esther gained the favor of Hegai and he readily gave her beauty preparations in addition to what she was supposed to receive, he also made sure that she had seven maidservants to tend her and gave her the best place in the house of the women. The bible explains,

***15** Now when the turn came for Esther the daughter of Abihail the uncle of Mordecai, who had taken her as his daughter, to go in to the king, she requested nothing but what Hegai the king's eunuch, the custodian of the women, advised. And Esther obtained favor in the sight of all who saw her. **17** The king loved Esther more than all the other women, and she obtained grace and favor in his sight more than all the virgins; so he set the royal crown upon her head and made her queen instead of Vashti. (Esther 2:15,17)*

HOLY SPIRIT WHISPERS

Since, we serve an all knowing God, He strategically placed Esther in the predestined location. He knew that this would prepare her for the purposes and plans He had for her. Throughout this process Esther remained humble and submitted to her uncle Mordecai, sought out the wisdom of Hegai, was highly favored and eventually chosen as queen. There is ALWAYS bigger picture than we can see. Just as discussed in Fearfully & Wonderfully Created, King David explains that God has knitted us together. When one knits they start out with a simple ball of yarn beginning by forming a chain stitch and it isn't until the patterns start forming together that the intended object can finally be realized. Gods providence placed Esther at the scene of the impeding genocide of the Jews. When approached by Mordecai for help, Esther responded by saying,

11 All the king's servants and the people of the king's provinces know that any man or woman who goes into the inner court to the king, who has not been called, he has but one law: put all to death, except the one to whom the king holds out the golden scepter, that he may live. Yet I myself have not been called to go in to the king these thirty days. (Esther 4:11)

Esther was met with the choice of facing death to potentially save her people or choosing to hide behind her newly gained position as queen. Esther, in the midst of uncertainty and fear, she called for a three day fast and made the declaration, **16** ...*If I perish, I perish."* (Esther 4:16)

We see that there were several invitations that Esther chose to accept, the obedience of her uncles request to remain silent about her heritage, the offer of the King to be Queen, the request of Mordecai to go before the King and the assignment to save her people. God fashions a plan and then seeks to see if we will submit to the plan He has for us. In our time of preparation we must stay close to recognize when God is on the move, we must walk in humility and obey the instructions given to us for victory. Gods divine helpers are all around to assist us through every phase of His plan. Esther had successfully walked through the process of preparation, taking on the necessary discipline and was able to save a nation. Just imagine if she had declined the invitation, what would have happened if the Jews were annihilated? It could have affected to entire bloodline of Jesus because Esther was actually King Davids niece.

Each of us must go through seasons of God's preparation for our purpose on earth to be fulfilled. Many are being prepared now even though you may not even be aware. All that you encounter in your life may not have been God's original plans for your life but He can certainly turn everything around to benefit you for good.

NOTES

Reflection Questions

In a quiet place reflect on what you are feeling, what stood out to you in this module and what the Lord spoke to you. Take some time to answer the questions below.

> DO YOU FEEL LIKE GOD HAS BEEN PREPARING YOU FOR SOMETHING BASED ON YOUR LIFE EXPERIENCES? IF YES, EXPLAIN. IF NO, BEGIN TO SEEK GOD ABOUT WHAT LIFE EXPERIENCES HE HAS USED TO GET YOU READY FOR HIS PLAN FOR YOU.

> DO YOU FEEL LIKE YOU HAVE WENT THROUGH THE PREPARATION PROCESS IN OBEDIENCE OR RESISTANCE?
> REFLECT ON YOUR EXPERIENCES, HAVE YOU GONE THROUGH THE SAME SITUATION MORE THAN ONCE? BE HONEST, IF SO BEGIN TO SEEK GOD ASKING WHAT IS NECESSARY TO PASS THIS PARTICULAR PHASE OF THE PREPARATION PROCESS.

Reflection Questions
CONTINUED

IS FEAR STOPPING YOU FROM WALKING INTO YOUR PURPOSE? IF SO, WHAT IS THE SOURCE OF THE FEAR- SEE PRAYER TREASURY

It's time to *MOVE forward!*

A great way to position yourself to clearly hear from God is by fasting. Fasting is where you abstain from food for a period of time to seek instructions from God. It is a spiritual discipline, you exchange the desire for natural food that feeds your body for spiritual food (prayer, bible reading). This puts the spiritual needs above the flesh, drawing you nearer to God. Once you begin to hear from God ask if there are any tangible tools that you may need to begin to step into destiny. Finally, pray about what areas that Lord has been preparing you to walk into. Do not make any assumptions in this arena, God most likely is doing something that you have no idea about.

Fast

Take a 1 to 3 day fast to seek God for instructions to prepare you for your next steps. The fast can be water only, liquids only or one meal a day. If you have medical conditions please check with your doctor and God to see what is best for you.

Seek

Begin to seek God to see if there are any tangible tools you may need to prepare for your destiny. For example, Education, training, supplies, transportation, collaborations etc.

Pray

Ask God what areas has He been preparing you in (Areas that you don't already know about)

BE FOUND DOING THE WILL OF
GOD, NO MATTER THE COST

...If I perish, I perish.

ESTHER 4:16

THE PROCESS OF PURPOSE

03

The Positioning

ARE YOU CURRENTLY POSITIONED FOR PURPOSE?
OFTEN YOU MAY FEEL AS THOUGH YOU ARE NOT,
HOWEVER, BY GOD'S PROVIDENCE, YOU ARE.

The Positioning

Many times we feel as though we are unable to fulfill the call of God on our lives because we believe that we don't have what it takes to carry out our destiny. We may feel that we don't have the skills necessary, the influence, the finances, the station in life or even the courage that is needed to stand firm against all odds. This module explains God's providence and how He positions people like you and I, makes provision for all the resources necessary and fills us with His Spirit giving us the courage, esteem and skills that are required for the fulfilling of our purpose.

PURPOSE OF THIS MODULE

- To realize that our inadequacies are insignificant to God

- To study examples of how God positions his people

- To discover how important details are to God

- To understand how God will strategically position you for destiny

Let's explore the history & lives of two men that were strategically positioned and used of God for a great purpose. Due to Israel's sin, King Nebuchadnezzar had taken the children of Israel into captivity, burned the city and the temple to the ground. After 70 years of captivity, Cyrus, the King conquered the Babylonians and allowed the Jews to return home from their exile to rebuild the temple & worship. We come in about 20 years after the Jews had come out of captivity, they were reestablishing the city, cultivating their lands, building their homes, but they had not yet completed the rebuilding of the temple of God. At the urging of the prophets Haggai & Zechariah, Zerubbabel & Joshua were tasked by God to rebuild the temple.

The prophet Haggai gives us a deeper look, as Joshua & Zerubbabel responded to the invitation with a resounding "Yes". The Lord stirred them up, promised them that He would not leave them and encouraged them not to fear. God also promised them that even though the temple did not look like much in its current state that the glory of the House of the Lord would be greater than even the first temple

6 For thus says the Lord of hosts: 'Once more (it is a little while) I will shake heaven and earth, the sea and dry land; 7 and I will shake all nations, and they shall come to the Desire of All Nations, and I will fill this temple with glory,' says the Lord of hosts.

8 'The silver is Mine, and the gold is Mine,' says the Lord of hosts. 9 'The glory of this latter temple shall be greater than the former,' says the Lord of hosts. 'And in this place I will give peace,' says the Lord of hosts." (Haggai 2:6-9)

The Governor

Zerubbabel was of the House of King David, which meant he was of the royal bloodline, as well as the governor of the rebuilt Jerusalem. The prophet Haggai, heard the words of the Lord in Haggai 2:20-23, clearly stating that He chose Zerubbabel for the purpose of leading the people and completing the rebuilding of the Temple. God showed Haggai that he had made Zerubbabel His signet ring. This was important because the signet is a seal used officially to give the bearer personal authority. In essence God was saying that He had ordered Zerubbabel's steps up unto this point and had given him the authority in the earth for the rebuilding the Temple.

Kindly note, this was a finishers anointing as will see later on.

Zerubbabel had laid the initial foundation of the Temple, however it had not been completed.

12 Then Zerubbabel the son of Shealtiel, and Joshua the son of Jehozadak, the high priest, with all the remnant of the people, obeyed the voice of the LORD their God, and the words of Haggai the prophet, as the LORD their God had sent him; and the people feared the presence of the LORD. 14 So the LORD stirred up the spirit of Zerubbabel the son of Shealtiel, governor of Judah, and the spirit of Joshua the son of Jehozadak, the high priest, and the spirit of all the remnant of the people; and they came and worked on the house of the LORD of hosts, their God. (Haggai 1:12,14)

The High Priest

God also positioned Joshua, son of Jehozadakin, in authority for the rebuilding of the Temple. He was a High Priest in the line of Aaron and appointed Levites to oversee the work of the Temple.

God gave the prophet Zechariah a vision regarding Joshua which was instrumental in confirming the plans God had for Joshua. As Joshua represented the priesthood, the people would come to him on the day of atonement to be cleansed of their sins. In Zechariah's vision (Zechariah 3:3-5), Joshua stands before the Angel of the Lord and satan. Satan stands ready to oppose Joshua, we know that satan is the accuser of the brethren. However, the first thing the Angel of the Lord does is rebukes satan! He then instructed those with Him to cleanse Joshua, removing his filthy garments thus taking away his sins.

In our next Module we will go deeper into the types and foreshadowing that explain a bigger picture of Zerubbabel and Joshua's positioning. However, it is crucial that we understand that God was concerned with the rebuilding of the temple but He was even more concerned about returning the hearts of the people back to Him. They had slipped into the sin of disobedience. Since Joshua, as the priest, represented the people before God, Zechariah's vision depicted the state of the people, the impeding legal right the enemy had to attack them due to their sin and the grace of God in sending His Son to take away the sins of not only the Jews but the world.

As we move into purpose it is crucial that we are vessels that God is able to use. He wants to cleanse, heal and pour His Spirit in us so that as we go out we can represent Him in all of His glory and power. His power is then available to bring transformation to the broken, sick and those in captivity. Our desire is to carry His presence to fulfill our purpose and to bring about results He planned from the beginning.

Before Joshua & Zerubbabel were born God had the distinct purpose in mind for the rebuilding of the temple. He intricately placed them in the specific blood lines that would allow them to be positioned to be in the governmental & religious sectors. They were both well known and honored among the people. They also came from the tribes that were designated by God to build the temple as well as care for the people of God. Their lives were predestined which led them to be in position when the time would come for the rebuilding of the temple. As mentioned earlier, God did not force or coerce them into fulfilling this predestined purpose, He gave them the choice just as He gives us. They could have said no, but as we see they both responded to the invitation with a resounding yes!

Reflection Questions

In a quiet place reflect on what you are feeling, what stood out to you in this module and what the Lord spoke to you. Take some time to answer the questions below.

HAVE YOU BEEN STAGNANT, NOT SEEING ANY GROWTH IN YOUR LIFE, MINISTRY, BUSINESS, DESTINY? EXPLAIN?

CAN YOU RELATE TO WHAT HAGGAI TOLD THE PEOPLE IN HAGGAI 1:3-11? HOW?

ARE YOU CURRENTLY IN A POSITION IN WHICH YOU HAVE AN OPPORTUNITY TO MAKE A GREAT IMPACT?

Reflection Questions
CONTINUED

WHAT HAVE YOU DONE WITH THE POSITION IN WHICH YOU HAVE BEEN PLACED?

LOOK BACK OVER YOUR LIFE, CAN YOU SEE WHERE GOD WAS POSITIONING YOU FOR PURPOSE? IF YES, EXPLAIN

It's time to *MOVE forward!*

Repentance helps us to re-align with purpose. The people had slipped into sin as they lived their newly re-established lives completely ignoring the instruction to build the temple. Make sure that you have not done anything that will hinder your forward progress in destiny. Secondly, it is crucial that we are in tune with what God is doing in the earth, pray as to whether or not you are positioned correctly at work, church or in business so that you are aligned with God's plans. Finally, it may be difficult to abandon the dreams you had for your life, all your life. God may have a different plan or even a different path to get you there. Ask God to give you the strength and capacity to align with His will for you.

Repent

Take some time to repent. Allow the Holy Spirit time to speak to areas of your life that are hindering your next move with God.

Pray

Begin to seek God to see if He is positioning in the natural or the Spirit for a greater purpose & if your current position is aligned with His purpose.

Ask

Ask God to help you to say "yes" to His purposes and plans for your life.

YOU ARE GOD'S SIGNET RING IN THE EARTH

…'I will take you, my servant Zerubbabel ..and I will make you like my signet ring, for I have chosen you…

HAGGAI 2:23

THE PROCESS OF PURPOSE

03

The Positioning pt. 2

GOD IS ALWAYS IN THE DETAILS, FOR THE BIGGER PICTURE. DO YOU HAVE HIS VISION?

The Positioning pt.2

As we look at the positioning of Zerubbabel & Joshua as well as the lives of the prophets whom God used to urge the rebuilding of the temple, we can start to see a bigger picture. Throughout the bible there are types and shadows of things to come. God uses symbols, visions, dreams and other means to point us to future promises. He does this to reassure us, give us vision for the future and help us to prepare and position ourselves for what's to come.

There was definitely a deeper message God was speaking in the details of what He was sharing with His people. We are going to dive a bit deeper, but first let's get an understanding. What is a type, shadow or symbol as it pertains to the Bible? A type, shadow, pattern, or figure is a prophetic foretelling of future events.[4]

PURPOSE OF THIS MOULE

- See from God's perspective

- To understand how God will always point to a greater purpose

God Is in the Details

God is truly in the details, we see here that He was concerned with every intricate detail about all those that were involved in the rebuilding of the temple. We can even see this in the names of the people He used for this great assignment. According to Wikipedia, Zerubbabel in Hebrew means seal and signet ring [5], the name Zechariah means God has remembered [6], Joshua means YHWH (God) is salvation [7], the name Haggai means my holiday (festive) [8]. As we examine this more closely we see that God used a prophet named Zechariah which means " Yahweh remembers" – to remind the people that He had never forgotten the promise He made that the temple would be rebuilt.

However, this was not just a promise of the rebuilding of the physical temple, it was a foreshadowing of the coming Messiah. God was also reminding His people that He would send yet another Temple, His Son Jesus. Remember, Jesus answered and said to them, "Destroy this temple, and in three days I will raise it up." *(John 2:19)* He also refers to this in Haggai, when he says, The glory of this latter house (Temple) shall be greater than of the former, saith the LORD of hosts: and in this place will I give peace, saith the LORD of hosts (Haggai 2:9). The glory of the Temple of the Lord would be much greater than any physical temple that they could ever build. God was reassuring them that He had not forgotten them in exile and that He had a vision for their future and that the coming of the Messiah was on the horizon.

HOLY SPIRIT WHISPERS

Even as Zerubbabel's name means seal & signet ring, God speaks to Haggai the prophet saying that He will take Zerubbabel His servant and make him a signet ring because He has chosen him (Haggai 2:23). We learned earlier that there was authority given with the signet, just as Jesus was given authority in the earth when He came as a man. Additionally, the role of Joshua, as the High Priest, was to make atonement of the peoples sins through a spotless lamb. In Zechariah's vision of Joshua, the one whose name means "YHWH is salvation", detailed how he stood before the Lord, depicting a literal picture of Jesus, the High Priest, taking away our sins.

Prophet, Priest & King

Let's dig a little deeper and see what other hidden gems we can unearth. Looking at the dynamics of God's chosen vessels we can clearly see the prefiguring of Jesus as Prophet, Priest & King. Both Zechariah & Haggai were prophets during that time. Every detail was precisely designed to point to Christ.

Joshua & Zerubabbel were not chosen by accident; they were specifically chosen to let the people know that God's promise to send Jesus would come to pass. Reading from Zechariah 6:11-13, God gives concise instructions for **crowns** to be made out of silver and gold. One crown was to be placed on the head of Joshua the High Priest.

Joshua was a High Priest, and was crowned as a type of Christ, who would be the Chief High Priest. Joshua was High Priest and now with the placement the crown on his head we see the shadow of Jesus Christ being both Priest and King. Just as Joshua was a builder of the temple, Jesus would be a Master builder.

The other crown was to be kept as a memorial (Zechariah 6:14) for the coming "BRANCH". We understand this BRANCH to be Jesus, as explained in this passage, who would be the Chief Captain of our salvation. God then directed Zechariah to speak to Joshua saying,"Behold the Man whose name is Branch! (Zechariah 6:12a)

We understand this BRANCH to be Jesus, as explained in this passage,

11 *There shall come forth a Rod from the stem of Jesse, and a Branch shall grow out of his roots.*

As we read further in the passage it says,

12 *And speak unto him, saying, Thus speaketh the LORD of hosts, saying, Behold the man whose name is The BRANCH; and he shall grow up out of his place, and he shall build the temple of the LORD:* **13** *Yes, He shall build the temple of the Lord. He shall bear the glory, And shall sit and rule on His throne; So He shall be a priest on His throne, And the counsel of peace shall be between them both.*

Zerubbabel was an ancestor of Christ, being of Royal bloodline and in government chosen to rebuild the temple. There are similarities between Jesus and Zerubbabel. Isaiah stated that the government would be on the shoulders of Jesus, meaning the government of the Kingdom of God (Isaiah 9:6). Just like Zerubbabel, Jesus was also a Repairer of Breach sent on assignment to repair what had been destroyed.

NOTES

12 *Those from among you, Shall build the old waste places; You shall raise up the foundations of many generations; And you shall be called the Repairer of the Breach, The Restorer of Streets to Dwell In. (Isaiah 58:12)*

The Royal blood of Zerubbabel shows forth the kingly anointing and authority of Jesus to right what is wrong and to bring the kingdom of heaven down in the earth. We also have a promise that just as Zerrubabel laid the foundation & would complete it, there is a finished work of Jesus Christ through the cross.

> HOLY SPIRIT WHISPERS

Ruling in the Earth

You may be asking, "What does this all mean for me NOW?" Zerubbabel & Joshua are also picture of us. Once we accept the invitation, have been prepared and are positioned we can walk in His FULL authority, chosen as his signet rings to fulfill our purpose & destiny here on earth. Joshua represents the priestly role of Jesus & Zerubabbel represents the Kingly role of Jesus that we now stand in on earth. *1 Peter 2:9 says,*

> 9 *"But you are not like that, for you are a chosen people. You are **royal priests**, a holy nation, God's very own possession.*
> ~1 Peter 2:9

As a result, you can show others the goodness of God, for He called you out of the darkness into his wonderful light. It is our assignment to understand and operate in our kingly role of authority and a priestly role to speak forth the Word of God here in the earth. These roles give us the positioning we need to walk out our purpose. Understanding your identity plays a major role in your confidence and assurity in Christ to step into your destiny.

Identity & confidence in Christ is crucial to walking in purpose. For example as a king or queen, would you walk around as a pauper? Absolutely NOT! If you know that you are royalty and possess a great level of authority, you would carry yourself in a posture of authority and power because you are ROYALTY! Often we perish for a lack of knowledge. (Hosea 4:6) We must know and live in our God given authority and identity.

You are Royalty, it's time that you Rule

— RENELE AWONO

Reflection Questions

In a quiet place reflect on what you are feeling, what stood out to you in this module and what the Lord spoke to you. Take some time to answer the questions below.

WHAT IS A TYPE, SHADOW, SYMBOL, FIGURE? WHY WAS THIS IMPORTANT DURING THE TIME OF EXILE?

LOOKING BACK OVER YOUR LIFE WHAT DETAILS CAN YOU SEE THAT GOD INTRICATELY PUT IN PLACE?

WHAT IS THE SIGNIFICANCE OF A SIGNET RING?

WHAT WAYS CAN YOU NOW WALK IN YOUR FULL GOD GIVEN AUTHORITY?

It's time to *MOVE forward!*

God has given us authority in the earth as discussed in this module, lacking full understanding of this can cripple us and prevent us from moving forward with full confidence as sons and daughters of the King. Take some time to seek out what has hindered you, as you discover those things, be mindful that some things that may be obvious to you and others that are hidden, but the Holy Spirit knows all things. Finally, take a look at the list of hinderances and develop, through prayer, a list of ways to overcome these hinderances. Let the Holy Spirit lead you in how to gain victory.

Seek

Research & Memorize five scriptures in the Bible that show where God has given you authority in the earth.

List

Make a list everything that has hindered you from walking in your full authority, then pray for the removal of everything on your list.

Overcome

Make a list of ways that you can **overcome** the obstacles that have kept you from walking in your authority.

STEP INTO HIS AUTHORITY

...You are a chosen people. You are royal priests, a holy nation, God's very own possession

1 PETER 2:9

THE PROCESS OF PURPOSE

The Purpose

04

WALKING IN YOUR GOD ORDAINED PURPOSE CRITICALLY IMPORTANT, BUT WHY?

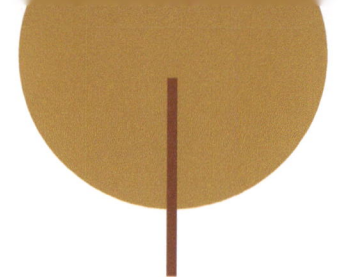

The Purpose

So what does walking out your purpose accomplish? After all, you may feel like you are one person in a sea of billions, asking yourself what difference can I make. Often, we talk ourselves out of being great because we feel insignificant. Many people believe that their contribution won't make that much of a difference so they just shrink back into their mundane lives, this could not be further from the truth!

PURPOSE OF THIS MODULE

- Discover what happens when we accept God's invitation

- To activate you into purpose

- To understand God's desire for your life

- To strengthen you in your pursuit of purpose

> **Wisdom is the principal thing; Therefore get wisdom. And in all your getting, get understanding**
>
> -PROVERBS 4:7

Often times our ignorance hinders us from fully coming into the manifestation of the glory of God in our lives. Walking into your destiny and living in the purpose you were created for is more weightier than you may have imagined. Let's dig into why you were created, why you were given His authority, and why it is imperative for you pursue your purpose, today!

TO PLEASE THE LORD

*Haggai 1:7-8 explains, "Thus says the Lord of hosts: "Consider your ways!" Go up to the mountain and bring wood and build my temple, that I may take **pleasure** in it and be glorified, "says the Lord.*

He has called us to a specific destiny and purpose, it will please Him to to see us doing what we were created to do.

TO MANIFEST GOD'S GLORY IN THE EARTH

This is the time in which He wants to bring the latter glory in the earth. Just as Zerubbabel & Joshua were tasked with building the temple, we are tasked with bringing the manifestation of His kingdom here on earth.

As we are walking in our purpose, co-laboring with Him we are those that bring the latter glory into the earth.

He is preparing us NOW so that we can be in position to receive and give out this glory in the earth.

> ## I Decree & Declare that I am a Craftsman sent by God to terrify the enemy!

TO SHOW FORTH GOD'S MANIFOLD WISDOM TO PRINCIPALITIES

To the intent that now unto the principalities and powers in heavenly places might be known by the church the manifold wisdom of God (Eph. 3:10)

As we use the gifting that God created us with we show forth the manifold wisdom of God to principalities.
(Manifold: multifaceted, many-colored)

We are showing forth the infinite ways that God uses His people and the infinite wisdom that God has over the enemy.

Some may be intercessors, some may wage war against the adversaries, some may receive critical revelation, some may be like the sons of Issachar discerning of the times and seasons.

The ways that God uses us to show forth His wisdom is innumerable.

TO TERRIFY THE ENEMY

*I asked the angel who was speaking to me, "What are these?" He answered me, "These are the horns that scattered Judah, Israel and Jerusalem." Then the Lord showed me four craftsmen. I asked, "What are these coming to do?" He answered, "These are the horns that scattered Judah so that no one could raise their head, but the **craftsmen** have come to **terrify** them and throw down these horns of the nations who lifted up their horns against the land of Judah to scatter its people." Zechariah 1:19-21*

The enemy has come against the church trying to cut off the name of Israel. As we operate, each of us in our own unique gifting, we terrify and throw satan down.

Notice how the word craftsmen is used here. It is an example of how God will use your gifts, talents, skills, wisdom, prayers to totally dismantle the enemy. God uses the manifold (many) colored ways that He operates through us to terrify the enemy.

As we walk out our purpose we please the Lord, manifest God's glory, show forth the manifold wisdom of God and terrify the enemy! We must be intentional about seeking out and stepping into our destinies. As you fill up, pour out and give out, things that may have held you in bondage can no longer keep its grip because you will begin to soar. Eagles see prey a far off, the swoop down, pick up their prey and then climb to unimaginable heights. Once they have reached their pinnacle, its prey has already met its demise because the prey cannot stand the altitude in which the eagle thrives. It's time for you to soar. You will also notice that small things that may have previously been irritants in your life just begin to roll off of your back, due to your pursuance of God's will for your life. There will be no time for those petty things which are not attached to destiny.

HOLY SPIRIT WHISPERS

Reflection Questions

In a quiet place reflect on what you are feeling, what stood out to you in this module and what the Lord spoke to you. Take some time to answer the questions below.

HOW DO WE SHOW PRINCIPALITIES & POWERS THE MANIFOLD WISDOM OF GOD?

WHO ARE THE CRAFTSMEN MENTIONED IN ZECHARIAH 1:21? WHAT IS THEIR PURPOSE?

NOW THAT YOU KNOW THE PURPOSE OF GOD'S "INVITATION", WHAT WILL YOU DO TO RECEIVE AND MANIFEST THE LATTER GLORY OF GOD HERE ON EARTH?

It's time to *MOVE forward!*

Walking in purpose must be intentional. Bill Johnson said, "you can have a measure of success in doing other things but when it comes to doing what you your were created for, there will be a fight." It is important that you move toward your purpose daily so that you can accomplish all that was discussed in this module. In all that we do we must be surrendered to God, this allows His plans & purposes to take shape in our lives. Lastly, research scriptures that propel you into destiny. Speaking the Word of God over your life is critical. The Word of God never goes out void, it always will work for you to accomplish that which is ordained by God.

Habit

Develop 3 daily habits that will propel you into the purpose that God has designed for you.

Pray

Pray the prayer of Surrender that listed in the Prayer Treasury.

List

Make a list of scriptures that back up God's purpose for your life and begin to declare them over your life.

THE PROCESS OF PURPOSE

**WALK IN YOUR PURPOSE &
TERRIFY THE ENEMY**

...but the craftsmen have come to terrify them and throw down these horns of the nations who lifted up their horns against the land of Judah to scatter its people...

ZECHARIAH 1:19-21

THE PROCESS OF PURPOSE

05

The Perfection

GOD HAS GIVEN US THE PERFECT EXAMPLE, JESUS. HE UNAPOLOGETICALLY WALKED OUT HIS PURPOSE AND SO CAN YOU.

The Perfection

Jesus gives us a flawless example of walking in purpose. Jesus was all God yet all man at the same time. His deity and humanity was captured by Paul in this passage, **9** *For in him the whole fullness of deity dwells bodily.* (Colossians 2:9) When He came down to earth as a man, He had a distinct purpose and began to fulfill that purpose from the time He was divinely placed in the womb of Mary.

7 *But made himself nothing, taking the form of a servant, being born in the likeness of men.* (Philippians 2:7) Even though the majority of what we see in scripture shows that Jesus began His ministry at thirty years of age, all throughout His life He was walking in destiny. Join me on a journey to glean from Jesus as He walked out His destiny here on earth.

PURPOSE OF THIS MODULE

- Introduce the Ultimate EXAMPLE of pursuing destiny
- Discover lessons from Jesus, to help you step into destiny
- To understand the providence of God

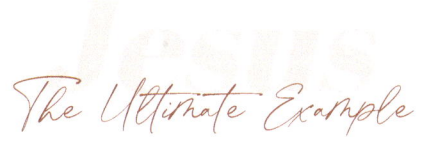

Jesus
The Ultimate Example

Jesus was born in Bethlehem, Biblical scholars believe Bethlehem, located in the "hill country" of Judah, may be the same as the Biblical Ephrath, which means "fertile", as there is a reference to it in the Book of Micah as Bethlehem Ephratah. The Bible also calls it Beth-Lehem Judah, and the New Testament describes it as the "City of David".[9] From His birth, the Bible explains that Jesus,

40... *grew and became strong in spirit, filled with wisdom and the grace of God was upon Him. (Luke 2:40)*

As a young child Jesus had a sense of purpose and accepted His invitation early in life, we understand this by His behavior at just twelve years old. Returning from an annual pilgrimage from Jerusalem, Mary & Joseph realized that Jesus was left behind. They went back only to find Jesus, three days later in the **46**...*temple sitting in the midst of the teachers, both listening and asking questions".(Luke 2:46)* When Mary asked Jesus why he had remained behind, His answer was, **49** *"Why did you seek Me? Did you not know that I MUST be about My Father's business? (Luke 2:49)* Jesus was in a season of preparation for His call. As a young adult Jesus was said to be carpenter, as His father Joseph was. It was common in that day for sons to take on the trades of their father's.

HOLY SPIRIT WHISPERS

As we take a closer look we see the prophetic prefiguring that as He was a builder then, He would later become the chief cornerstone, the foundation, the One upon which everything would be built.

6 See, I lay a stone in Zion, a chosen and precious cornerstone, and the one who trusts in him will never be put to shame. (1 Peter 2:6)

Jesus, at the age of 30, was yet being prepared for His ministry when He was led by Spirit into the wilderness. He spent forty days fasting and being tempted of the devil until the time His preparation would be completed,

14 Then Jesus returned to Galilee, filled with the Holy Spirit's power. Reports about him spread quickly through the whole region. (Luke 4:14)

When His season of preparation was ended we see that He came out being filled with the power of the Holy Spirit this was a result of allowing God's process of preparation over His life to take its full course. God is so intentional with our lives and He never makes a mistake.

NOTES

Jesus was born of a virgin, which was crucial to the maintenance of His deity. He would not have been able to deemed the Son of God if born through human seed.

THE BLOODLINE BLESSING

In that same vein, if we dig deeper into the bloodline of Jesus Christ we see that although Joseph was not the "natural" father of Jesus, he was His legal father. Therefore, He carried the name and bloodline of Joseph which placed Jesus in the line of David. A glimpse of the genealogy of Jesus Christ laid out below (abbreviated here)

Abraham begot Isaac... Isaac begot Jacob... Obed begot Jesse...Jesse begot David the King...Sheatiel begot Zerubbabel...Jacob begot Joseph the husband to Mary, of whom was born Jesus the Christ (Matthew 1:2,5,6,12,16)

Being in David's bloodline was critical because God's promise was that David's offspring would rule on the throne forever, in a natural sense & spiritual sense. (2 Samuel 7) This also speaks prophetically to Jesus, to whose Kingdom there is no end.

33 *And he shall reign over the house of Jacob for ever; and of his Kingdom there shall be no end. (Luke 1:33)*

This gives us a glimpse of one of the ways that Jesus was positioned by God to fulfill His destiny. As we have traced back the bloodline of Jesus I want to draw your attention to Zerubbabel. We discussed earlier that he was also in the bloodline of David, as noted in Zechariah,

9 *"The hands of Zerubbabel have laid the foundation of this temple; his hands will also complete it. Then you will know that the LORD Almighty has sent me to you. Zerubbabel laid the foundation of the Temple. (Zechariah 4:9)*

Isn't it interesting that Zerubbabel, having laid the foundation of the Temple & being royalty in the line of David, would be the prophetic prefiguring to Christ, who is the foundation upon which everything else is built.

JESUS' PURPOSE IN A NUTSHELL

Scripture points us to Jesus' purpose, which was clearly defined.

10 For the Son of Man has come t**o seek and to save that which was lost.** (Luke 19:10)

18 The Spirit of the Lord is upon me, because he hath anointed me to **preach the gospel to the poor; he hath sent me to heal the brokenhearted, to preach deliverance to the captives, and recovering of sight to the blind, to set at liberty them that are bruised, 19 To preach the acceptable year of the Lord.** (Luke 4:18-19)

1 Look at my servant, whom I strengthen. He is my chosen one, who pleases me. I have put my Spirit upon him. He will **bring justice to the nations.** *(Isaiah 42:1)*

18 For Christ also suffered once for sins, the righteous for the unrighteous, that he might **bring us to God, being put to death in the flesh but made alive in the spirit.**
(1 Peter 3:18)

8 Son though he was, he learned obedience from what he suffered 9 and, once made perfect, **he became the source of eternal salvation for all who obey him.**
(Hebrews 5:8-9)

NOTES

Lessons in Purpose

So what lessons can we learn from how Jesus walked out His purpose? How did Jesus walk out His purpose?
He knew what His purpose was and was intentional about fulfilling it. Jesus was so purpose driven that He followed the destiny that was given to Him even though it meant death. Come what may, be disciplined and determined to be & do all that a God created you for.

8 And being found in appearance as a man, He humbled Himself and became obedient to the point of death, even the death of the cross. (Philippians 2:8)

HE UNDERSTOOD THAT HIS PURPOSE WAS PREORDAINED

There are books in heaven where our names are written and everything about out lives are laid out as mentioned earlier in Psalms 139:16.

Jesus knew this and was intentional about completing all that had been written of Him beforehand.

7 Then said I, Lo, I come (in the volume of the book it is written of me, to do thy will, O God. (Hebrews 10:7)

HE UNDERSTOOD THE TIMING OF WHEN HIS MINISTRY SHOULD BEGIN

Timing is important to God, it is crucial to move in rhythm and in step with God. The bible explains that,

32 And of the children of Issachar, which were men that had understanding of the times, to know what Israel ought to do; the heads of them were two hundred; and all their brethren were at their commandment.
(1 Chronicles 12:32)

Here Jesus knew that it was not yet time for His ministry to begin, even though He honored His mothers request.

4 Jesus said to her, "Woman, what does your concern have to do with Me? My hour has not yet come." (John 2:4)

HE UNDERSTOOD HIS MISSION TO THE APOSTLES

As a leader and teacher He cast vision for the apostles that enabled them to see further than what was happening while He was with them. As we walk out our destiny it may include preparing others for what's to come in various facets of life, ministry, marketplace dynamics, in the nation and beyond.

2 And Jesus said to them, "Do you not see all these things? Assuredly, I say to you, not one stone shall be left here upon another, that shall not be thrown down." 3 Now as He sat on the Mount of Olives, the disciples came to Him privately, saying, "Tell us, when will these things be? And what will be the sign of Your coming, and of the end of the age? (Matthew 24:2-3)

HE HAD GREAT FAITH

Jesus exhibited great faith. It takes faith to step into your destiny, there may time in which you cannot see where you are heading but your faith in God will lead you to where you should be in that season.

22-24 And Jesus answered them, "Have faith in God. Truly, I say to you, whoever says to this mountain, 'Be taken up and thrown into the sea,' and does not doubt in his heart, but believes that what he says will come to pass, it will be done for him. Therefore I tell you, whatever you ask in prayer, believe that you have received it, and it will be yours. (Mark 11:22-24)

HE UNDERSTOOD THE POWER & NECESSITY OF PRAYER

He was persistent in prayer while displaying the importance of His relationship with God the Father. Consistent intimacy in prayer with the Father will help you to know Him on a deeper level, which will increase your faith

& trust in Him as well as help you to tap into the instructions on how to fulfill your destiny.

1 And he spake a parable unto them to this end, that men ought always to pray, and not to faint; (Luke 18:1)

HE KNEW THE WORD OF GOD

He knew how to tap into the Word of God to overcome satan. Hebrews 4:12 explains,

12 For the word of God is quick, and powerful, and sharper than any two edged sword, piercing even to the dividing asunder of soul and spirit, and of the joints and marrow, and is a discerner of the thoughts and intents of the heart.

5 Then the devil taketh him up into the holy city, and setteth him on a pinnacle of the temple, 6 And saith unto him, If thou be the Son of God, cast thyself down: for it is written, He shall give his angels charge concerning thee: and in [their] hands they shall bear thee up, lest at any time thou dash thy foot against a stone. 7 Jesus said unto him, It is written again, Thou shalt not tempt the Lord thy God. (Matthew 4:5-7)

HE WAS FULL OF THE HOLY SPIRIT & POWER

Jesus operated in power demonstrating miracles, signs & wonders. His relationship with the Father strengthened Him in power. Jesus said,

12 Verily, verily, I say unto you, He that believeth on me, the works that I do shall he do. (John 14:12)

22 Men of Israel, hear these words: Jesus of Nazareth, a man attested to you by God with mighty works and wonders and signs that God did through him in your midst, as you yourselves know (Acts 2:22)

HE SOUGHT TO PLEASE THE FATHER

He was definitely a God pleaser as opposed to being a people pleaser.

As you walk out your destiny there will be people that don't agree with what you are doing. Just as Jesus did, set your face like a flint and do what you were created to do!

43 "You have heard that it was said, 'You shall love your neighbor and hate your enemy. 44 But I say to you, love your enemies, bless those who curse you, do good to those who hate you, and pray for those who spitefully use you and persecute you, 45 That ye may be the children of your Father which is in heaven: for he maketh his sun to rise on the evil and on the good, and sendeth rain on the just and on the unjust. (Matthew 5:43-45)

Jesus was explaining that there was a new & living way. You may be positioned by God as a pioneer, move forward in accordance with God's plans, even if it means going against the traditional ways.

HE WAS PERSISTENT IN THE MIDST OF PERSECUTION

He was diligent even in the face of persecution from the religious leaders of His time. Almost everything that Jesus was sent to do contradicted the religious culture of His day.

However, He walked in truth and completed His assignment unapologetically.

17 Tell us therefore, What thinkest thou? Is it lawful to give tribute unto Caesar, or not. 18 But Jesus perceived their wickedness, and said, Why tempt ye me, ye hypocrites? 19 Shew me the tribute money. And they brought unto him a penny. 20 And he saith unto them, Whose is this image and superscription? 21 They say unto him, Caesar's. Then saith he unto them, Render therefore unto Caesar the things which are Caesar's; and unto God the things that are God's. (Matthew 22:17-21)

HE HAD FULL CONFIDENCE IN HIS FATHER

He was not fearful and had unwavering confidence in His heavenly Father. Jesus knew that fear was not from His Father therefore, He did not allow it to cripple Him. Put your trust in God, taking every concern to Him in prayer.

20 For the Father loves the Son and shows him all he does. Yes, and he will show him even greater works than these, so that you will be amazed. (John 5:20)

HIS PURPOSE WAS OF THE UTMOST PRIORITY

He prayed to overcome His flesh, when faced with the most difficult time of His life, the crucifixion. There are things in our lives that will try to hinder us from walking out our purpose, we have to seek God for the grace to overcome those obstacles.

36 *And He said, "Abba, Father, all things are possible for You. Take this cup away from Me; nevertheless, not what I will, but what You will." (Mark 14:36)*

Everything necessary for the fulfillment of God's blueprint in the life of Jesus was already on the inside of Him. He accepted the invitation and sought His Father for every step He took. Jesus maintained a posture of obedience.

19 *Very truly I tell you, the Son can do nothing by himself; he can do only what he sees his Father doing, because whatever the Father does the Son also does. (John 5:19)*

NOTES

Perfect Implementation

God gave us the gift of the perfect example, Jesus, to help us to step into our destiny. Just as we have seen throughout the life of Jesus, God has gone to every length to weave purpose and destiny into the fabric of our lives whether we have the full picture or not. He is so detailed and through His providence in our lives no stone will be left unturned.

Additionally as we look at the life of Jesus we see that **He pleased the Lord**,

5 While he yet spake, behold, a bright cloud overshadowed them: and behold a voice out of the cloud, which said, This is my beloved Son, in whom I am well pleased; hear ye him. (Matthew 17:5)

He manifested the glory of God in the earth through many miracles, signs and wonders, John expressed it this way,

14 And the Word became flesh and dwelt among us, and we have seen his glory, glory as of the only Son from the Father, full of grace and truth. (John 1:14)

Jesus exhibited God's manifold wisdom to principalities and powers by coming in the form of a man and defeating every enemy and overcoming every temptation all without sin as found here in 1 Peter 21-22;

21 For even hereunto were ye called: because Christ also suffered for us, leaving us an example, that ye should follow his steps: 22 Who did no sin, neither was guile found in his mouth.

Finally, ***Jesus was a terror to the enemy*** (satan & the religious leaders), the religious leaders sought to kill Him and according to Revelation 1:18,

18 Jesus says, I am the Living One; I was dead, and now look, I am alive for ever and ever! And I hold the keys of death and Hades.

The keys represent power & authority, He took power and authority from the kingdom of darkness! Jesus is our perfect example, made in the likeness of Him, we are to walk out our purpose in that same way!

Reflection Questions

In a quiet place reflect on what you are feeling, what stood out to you in this module and what the Lord spoke to you. Take some time to answer the questions below.

WHOSE BLOODLINE WAS JESUS CONNECTED TO THAT PLACED HIM IN THE LINE OF DAVID?

WHAT LESSONS DID JESUS SHOW WHILE WALKING OUT HIS PURPOSE THAT YOU FEEL YOU NEED TO IMPLEMENT IN YOUR LIFE?

HAS GOD EVER SHOWED YOU GLIMPSES OF DESTINY IN YOUR LIFE PRIOR TO YOU HAVING THE FULL MANIFESTATION OF THEM? IF YES, EXPLAIN.

WHAT DO YOU FEEL IS YOUR MOST DIFFICULT CHALLENGE WHEN IT COMES TO STEPPING INTO DESTINY?

It's time to *MOVE forward!*

Just as Jesus walked out His purpose in perfection, we have the same opportunity to learn from His example. At times we may find it difficult to move into the destiny that God preordained for us. Take some time to pray asking for the help of the Holy Spirit to move into purpose. We are in a season now where we must find grace & strength in the Lord to do all and be all He created us to be. Along life's path we all have, no doubt, ran into issues and circumstances that may have taken us away from the will of God for our destinies. It's time to realign with His example, making sure that there are no roadblocks in the way. Develop intentional habits that help you to walk out your destiny using lessons that Jesus gave us, being full of faith and confident that He is with you.

Pray

Pray the prayer to follow Jesus' example in walking out your destiny.

Reflect

Ask yourself what character traits inside of you that may be a hinderance to aligning with Jesus example. Make a list and begin to ask for God's help daily to remove these out of your life.

Practice

Learn & study other ways Jesus walked out His destiny and make those practices a part of your everyday life.

WALK OUT YOUR PURPOSE...
IT IS EVERYTHING

And being found in appearance as a man, He humbled Himself and became obedient to the point of death, even the death of the cross.

PHILIPPIANS 2:8

THE PROCESS OF PURPOSE

The Response

IT'S TIME TO ANSWER THE CALL ON YOUR LIFE, RSVP TODAY!

06

The Response

As we reflect on our study, each person was used by God in a tremendous way to fulfill the agenda of the Kingdom of God. We often miss the fact that God is doing a far greater work in us than we can imagine. Generally, we see things on a micro level however, God works on the micro level. He moves with the understanding of how every piece will connect and fit together perfectly.

If we take an even deeper look still, Isaiah was used by God to predict the coming of the Messiah as the Ultimate leader, Esther was used as well, in fact, she thwarted the plans of the enemy to cut off the life of the Messiah. This assassination attempt was planned by the adversary long before Jesus even entered the earth.

PURPOSE OF THIS MODULE

- Provoke you to action

- Open your eyes to the Bigger Picture

- To help you to see that He intentionally included you in His plan

You see, Esther was a direct descendant of Jesse; her uncle was King David, as we discussed earlier Jesus was in the bloodline of King David. If the Jews would have gotten annihilated at that point Jesus would not have made it on the scene.

The plan for genocide of the Jews even goes back further. If we peek into the bloodline of Haman, we will find that he was a descendant of Agag, king of the Amalekites. The Amalekites were sworn enemies of the Jews. King Saul had disobeyed the commandment of the Lord to kill all of the Amalekites, instead he kept King Agag alive. Obedience to purpose is critical, because of Sauls disobedience generations later the life & destiny of the Messiah was threatened.

Contemplating on our study, we understand that in the bloodline of David, Zerubbabel & Joshua (foreshadows) were promises of hope to the people that the Messiah would come. When Jesus, the Messiah did come on the scene, He was a disrupter! He came to accomplish His purpose on earth with out apology. I love the fact that Jesus was a disrupter of the norm, of the things that a were in direct opposition to the kingdom of God. I am sure that it was not easy going against the flow of the cultural traditions of that day. However, look how the apostles turned the world upside down, or right side up!

HOLY SPIRIT WHISPERS

Let's take a final look at Joshua and Zerubbabel. Take some time to read Zechariah chapter 4 before moving on, this will give you an understanding as we move into the final portion of our bible study. There are some key components that we don't want to miss as we take a look at the practical application of this text to your life.

In walking out our purpose we must understand that we are assured victory. *Zechariah 4: explains, So he said to me, "This is the word of the Lord to Zerubbabel: 'Not by might nor by power, but by my Spirit,' says the Lord Almighty.* The angel was showing Zechariah a picture of how Zerubbabel would be victorious, only when he relied on the Spirit of God. We cannot do ANYTHING on our own or even with the help of many, we need the power of the Holy Spirit to do ALL that He created us to do.

In Zechariah 4:2-3 & 11-14, we see that there were olive trees that were draining into the bowls, this shows forth an endless supply of the oil, which depicts the Holy Spirit. The oil represented the endless supply of what Zerubbabel & Joshua would need to complete their assignment. The fact that Zerubbabel & Joshua were named the "sons of oil; anointed ones, lets us know that they took full advantage of the anointing that was available to them.

In the same manner we need to tap into the endless supply of the Holy Spirit which guarantees victory & success as we walk out our purpose.

We know that victory was assured as we look at Zechariah 4:7-10. Although there would be obstacles and the task of rebuilding seemed insurmountable, God assured him that it would be completed. Verse 9 explains that God had used Zerubbabel to start the work & He would also use him to complete it by the help of the Lord. There may be things that you have started and gave up midway through but God is calling for you to finish the work that you were created to do and receive the victory.

Finally, God shows Zechariah something very significant. As we examine verse 10 of Zechariah chapter 4, we see that a warning is given not to despise the day of small things.

> **Don't despise the day of small things, they rejoiced just to see the plumbline in the hand of Zerubbabel.**
>
> ~Zechariah 4:10

You may think that what you are doing, as you begin to walk in purpose is insignificant, however it's made very clear in this scripture that nothing you do for Christ is inconsequential.

Zechariah's vision draws us to a seemingly insignificant object called a plumbline. A plumbline is a tool that is important for lining up anatomical geometries and visualizing the subject's center of balance [10], it's a tool used in construction. Zechariah calls our attention to the fact that as soon as the plumline was in Zerubbabel's hand, the eyes of the Lord looked and He was pleased. Since Zerubbabel was building the Temple it made sense that he would be using this tool. God was making it absolutely clear that when Zerubbabel picked up the first tool to move into his purpose, the Lord was pleased! It is the same with you and I, as soon as we say yes and begin to step into destiny, the Lord rejoices.

The work was ordained by God. Zerubbabel had the Kingly & Priestly authority to carry out the destiny in the earth that was preordained for him. By the endless supply of the Holy Spirit Zerubbabel would be inspired, this is the same for you and I.

> **No matter where you begin in walking out your purpose, one of the most important things is that you take action!**
>
> -Renele Awono

Reflection Questions

In a quiet place reflect on what you are feeling, what stood out to you in this module and what the Lord spoke to you. Take some time to answer the questions below.

HAVE YOU RSVP'D YET? YES OR NO, IF NOT WHY?

IN WHAT SECTOR OR INDUSTRY DO YOU FEEL CALLED? RELIGIOUS, EDUCATION, ARTS & ENTERTAINMENT, GOVERNMENT, MEDIA, ARTS & ENTERTAINMENT, BUSINESS, AND FAMILY.

WHAT PEOPLE GROUP ARE YOU CALLED TO? CHURCHED, WOMEN, DISADVANTAGED, ENTERTAINERS, 7 FIGURE EARNERS, MEN, CHILDREN, ETC.?

It's time to *MOVE forward!*

What will you do? Will you accept the invitation that you have been given to fulfill your destiny? Now is the time to begin to move toward what God intended for your life from the beginning of time. Take a moment and write down the first action that you will do to begin moving toward your destiny. Reflect on solutions that you can implement that will assist you in walking into purpose. Lastly, pray for God to give you His wisdom. Wisdom will help you to move with ease and clarity, giving you instructions that lead you as you partner with the Holy Spirit as God purposed from the beginning.

Take Action

Write the first action that you will take toward your destiny

Reflect

Take a moment to develop solutions to obstacles that may stand the way of walking out your destiny. This will help you when obstacles arise, you will already have a solution.

Pray

Pray the prayer for Wisdom in the Prayer Treasury

STEP INTO WHAT YOU WERE CREATED FOR KNOWING GOD SAYS THIS ABOUT YOUR FUTURE

For I know the thoughts that I think toward you, says the Lord, thoughts of peace and not of evil, to give you a future and a hope.

JEREMIAH 29:11

THE PROCESS OF PURPOSE

7 Day Purpose Challenge

Pray for clarity of Purpose

CHALLENGE DAY 1
SEEK GOD TO GET CLEAR ON WHAT YOUR PURPOSE IS. ASK HIM TO CONFIRM, HIS WORD REGARDING YOUR PURPOSE

What do you have?

CHALLENGE DAY 2
SEEK OUT WHAT YOU ALREADY HAVE THAT SPEAKS TO YOUR PURPOSE. THIS MAY BE SKILLS, SPIRITUAL GIFTS, TANGIBLE OR INTANGIBLE ITEMS, RELATIONSHIPS OR INFLUENCE

Listen for instructions

CHALLENGE DAY 3
SPEND TODAY SEEKING GOD FOR INSTRUCTIONS ON WHERE TO BEGIN IN WALKING OUT YOUR PURPOSE

Write the Vision

CHALLENGE DAY 4
WITHOUT A VISION THE PEOPLE PERISH. LET THE HOLY SPIRIT INSPIRE YOU TO WRITE DOWN THE VISION / STRATEGY FOR YOUR PURPOSE

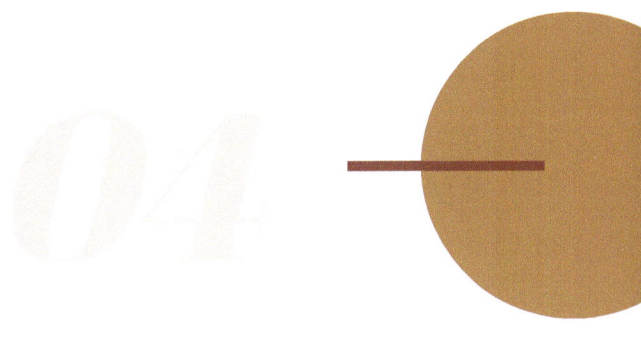

Plan your Purpose

CHALLENGE DAY 5
SET AND CALENDAR ACTIONABLE GOALS WITH REALISTIC DEADLINES.
ACTIONABLE GOALS: SMALL OBJECTIVES TO CARRY OUT THAT WILL ASSIST YOU IN ACCOMPLISHING YOUR PURPOSE

Pray. Pray. Pray.

CHALLENGE DAY 6
PRAY FOR THE STRENGTH, THE CAPACITY, THE RESOURCES, THE FAVOR, THE HUMILITY AND ALL IT WILL TAKE TO ACCOMPLISH YOUR PURPOSE. PRAY AGAINST, DELAY, PROCRASTINATION, CONFUSION AND ANY OTHER DESTINY THEIF.

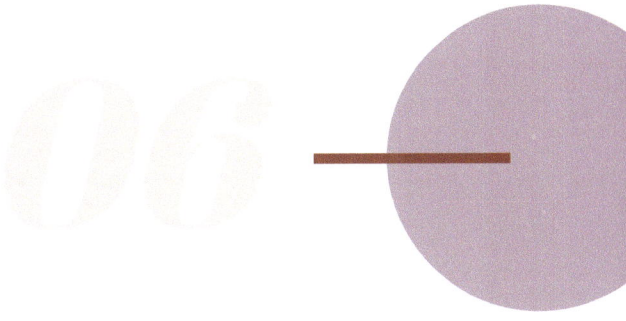

Move toward Purpose

CHALLENGE DAY 7
TAKE ACTION ON WHAT GOD HAS SPOKEN TO YOU. BEGIN TO COMPLETE EACH TASK, REMAINING OPEN TO THE LEADING OF THE HOLY SPIRIT.

Prayer *Treasury*

The following prayer prompts have been designed for you to use throughout your journey of discovering purpose, seeking God & planning. They are an invitation into deeper level of prayer and developing a closer relationship with your Creator.

GRACE TO ACCEPT THE INVITATION

I may not know what you have designed for my life, but today I accept your invitation. Forgive me for being afraid to say yes, for making excuses and previously choosing not to respond to your invitation. I choose to take a leap of faith and step into what you created me for. Fear will not hinder me in this season from laying hold to all that God has in store for my family, finances, ministry, destiny and myself in Jesus name... Amen

SALVATION

Lord, I know that I have not accepted you, today is the day. I chose to release all of the things that have held me down, I give them to you. Every form of sin and disobedience in my life I repent, reject and renounce it. I accept you into my heart and ask for your help in leading my life from this point on in Jesus name... Amen

GROWTH

God I thank you that you say, " ask and you shall receive, " I am asking for results, I don't want to be stagnant I want to GROW. I cancel every hinderance and assignment against my life for delay and bondage. I cancel any form of death and abortion meant to kill my destiny, drive, my forward progress and my passion in Jesus name. I decree and declare that ALL that God has created me for shall come to pass! I will not miss any project or mantle that God wants to give me in Jesus name... Amen.

IDENTITY

Lord thank you for calling me before I was even born (Jeremiah 1). I want to have a full understanding of who I am in you. Please show me who you created me to be. Please remove anything in me that you did not put there (Matthew 15:13) Grant me the grace to see me as you designed me to be in Jesus name...Amen

CONTINUED

WISDOM

Lord, I am asking you for wisdom, you said in that if any man lacks wisdom he can ask for it and you will freely give it to him (James 1:5). I am asking for the wisdom I need to walk out the destiny you designed for me. I'm seeking wisdom to help me to effectively carry out every detail of your plan for my life in Jesus name... Amen

OBEDIENCE

I repent for any disobedience in my life that has kept me from growing and moving forward in you. Your Word says that, **13** There hath no temptation taken you but such as is common to man: but God is faithful, who will not suffer you to be tempted above that ye are able; but will with the temptation also make a way to escape, that ye may be able to bear it. (1 Corinthians 10:13) God give me the grace to overcome any temptation for me to be disobedient. I decree and declare I am obedient in Jesus name.

AGAINST FEAR

Lord you said in the Word, that you have not given me a spirit of fear...(2 Timothy 1:7). I repent for aligning myself with something that you have not given me and I renounce and reject fear. I decree and declare that I am full of faith, the God kind of faith that moves mountains (Matthew 21:21). Lord help me to no longer partner with fear in my life, instead help me to walk in power, love and a sound mind in Jesus name... Amen

PURPOSE

Lord, I am not quite sure what my purpose is but I pray that you will give me clarity. I thank you for helping me thus far, I would like to now surrender the entire purpose for my life over to you. Until now I have operated on my own, wandering back and forth trying to find out what I was here for. Help me to walk out your specific purposes as explained here and outlined in your Word. Allow me to see clearly what that means for me. You have permission to change my mind sets, understanding and ways of thinking to align with yours. Give me a deeper understanding of your love for me in the name of Jesus...Amen

Prayer Treasury
CONTINUED

TO FOLLOW JESUS' EXAMPLE

Lord, I want to walk out the purpose you have given me according to the example that Jesus left for us. Help me to complete my assignment in the boldness and courage Jesus had. Help me to get close to the Father so that I will only do what the Father is asking me to do. Help my life to be transformed and to bring transformation to many. Let me be a sign & a wonder, a demonstration of your power on earth. I decree and declare that I will be ALL that you created me to be from the beginning of time in Jesus name... Amen

SURRENDER

Lord I give up, I am waving the white flag, I surrender. I give you my life, my will, my family, my control. Guide me and give me directions on how to live this life. I believe that you will for me life is best. I am asking for your grace to help me out of my current challenges and move me into the life you choose for me. Thank you for your loving kindness. I repent for trying to do this on my own, I repent for stubbornness & disobedience. Help me to remain in the posture of surrender, humility & gratitude. Thank you for opening your arms to accept me as I am and giving me the grace to mature into the son/daughter you created me to be in the name of Jesus...Amen

CLARITY

Lord, I thank you because you are not the author of confusion (1 Corinthians 14:33). Therefore, I pray clarity and understanding of your timing & purposes in my life. I pray that you give me the understanding of what to do and knowledge about the times/seasons of the Lord, like the children of Issachar (1 Chronicles 12:32). I thank you for clear vision to see and accurate perception as I walk out the things that you have created me to do in the earth in Jesus name....Amen

COMPASSION & LOVE

Lord, I thank you for showing compassion & mercy to me in times of my greatest brokenness. You reached for me out of heart of deep compassion and love to heal & strengthen me in ways I could never do for myself. You compassion has worked miracles for others. Help me to be sensitive & compassionate enough to feel your heart for others. Help me be open to your heart in wanting to reach those that need a touch from the loving Father in Jesus name....Amen

THE PROCESS OF PURPOSE

> **Pursue Your Purpose! You can start late, look different, be uncertain and still succeed.**

NOTES

1. "Purpose." dictionary.com , dictinary.com, www.dictionary.com/browse/purpose. Accessed 29, December 2020

2. "Calling." dictionary.com , dictinary.com, www.dictionary.com/browse/calling. Accessed 15, December 2020

3. Article: The Lord God …Before Whom I Stand (Part 2), Lee Ann Rubsam, https://refinedinthefire.wordpress.com/2007/10/08/the-lord-god-before-whom-i-stand-part-2/, Accessed 28, December 2020

4. Article:Types, shadows, patterns and figures in the Bible., https://www.bibletruths.org/types-shadows-patterns-figures-in-the-bible/ Accessed 8 January 2021

5. Article: Zerubbabel, https://en.wikipedia.org/wiki/Zerubbabel, Accessed 8 January 2021

6. Article: Zechariah, https://en.wikipedia.org/wiki/Zechariah_(given_name)#:~:text=Zechariah%2C%20also%20transliterated%20as%20Zachariah,the%20names%20of%20the%20God. Accessed 8 January 2021

7. Article: Joshua, https://en.wikipedia.org/wiki/Joshua_(name), Accessed 8 January 2021

8. Article: Haggai, https://en.wikipedia.org/wiki/Haggai, Accessed 8 January 2021

9. Article: Bethlehem, https://en.wikipedia.org/wiki/Bethlehem, Accessed 11 January 2021

10. Article: Plumbline, https://findanyanswer.com/what-is-plumb-line-in-physics, Accessed 12 May 2021

ABOUT THE AUTHOR

Renele Awono is a happily married mother of three, who lives on the West Coast. Psalms 139:14 has been her confession, long before she had the true sense of its meaning. It is her deepest desire to catch up to all God created her to be, daily she walks out this journey one step at a time. If you have not noticed already, Renele is a strong woman of faith, who believes that intentional pursuit of one's purpose is essential.

On her journey, she has obtained her Associates of Arts Degree in Liberal Arts, Bachelor's Degree in Business Administration with a focus on International Business. She has also earned a Minor Degree in Spanish and is studying, the language of love, French. Renele is a humanitarian at heart and throughout her life has sought out opportunities to serve those in need. In addition, she has worked in several industry sectors including nonprofit, local & foreign governments.

In pursuit of her destiny, Renele intends to assist others in seeking out all that they were created to be!

Fearfully & Wonderfully Created
English, Spanish & French

You were created & masterfully designed to fulfill God's purpose. That means that you were not an accident!

Fearfully & Wonderfully Created can be purchased on Amazon or the website. Take some time to check out other products & services by Renele Awono.

WWW.RENELEAWONO.COM

www.ingramcontent.com/pod-product-compliance
Lightning Source LLC
Chambersburg PA
CBHW042007150426
43195CB00002B/46